Turtle Tide

The Ways of Sea Turtles

To Allison—

I ♡ Sea Turtles!

By Stephen R. Swinburne   Illustrated by Bruce Hiscock

Boyds Mills Press
Honesdale, Pennsylvania

Steve Swinburne —2013

T HE MOTHER SEA TURTLE swam on and on through the dark sea, pulled by a great longing to come ashore. To leave the safety of the water was strange — her life had been spent in the open ocean. But she knew she must lay her eggs in a sandy nest. She moved closer and closer to the long, silent coast.

The sea turtle rose to the surface to breathe. The beach was near. She could hear the surf and see a long ridge of high dunes in the early evening light. She raised her nose above the waves and smelled the wind coming off the shore.

She swam hard and rode the incoming wave. The sea charged onto the beach. She crawled out of the surf and lowered her beak into the wet sand. She remembered this place; she remembered the beach. This was the windswept Atlantic coast where she had been born many years ago.

She felt awkward on land. She used her front flippers to heave her body step by step to the high-tide line. Her breathing came in deep hollow gasps. She inched forward a few steps and stopped. She lifted her head and gazed down the beach as if she saw something, as if she heard something. She was very cautious.

The sea turtle found her spot and settled her large body into the soft dune. She faced away from the sea and began digging a hole with her hind limbs. Each paddle-shaped flipper scooped sand and flung it away from the hole. Sand flew into her face, and tears rinsed salt and sand from her eyes.

Her hind flippers reached as far down as they could. She made the hole wide at the bottom and narrow at the top, like the shape of a vase. She rested her chin in the dune and exhaled loudly. The hole was finished.

Without looking back once, she began laying eggs — leathery, cream-colored eggs the size of Ping-Pong balls. They dropped in ones, twos, and threes, wet and glistening in the light of a rising full moon. Her shell, covered with ancient barnacles and seaweed, heaved silently.

Once she began to lay eggs, the sea turtle would not stop, could not stop. Tears flooded her eyes. She raised her head slightly every time an egg came as if she wanted to see what was falling from her. The eggs piled up. Ten. Twenty. Sixty. One hundred.

The mother turtle wasted no time before covering her eggs — her rear flippers pushed sand into the opening. She shifted from side to side and worked herself over the nest site. Her weight packed down the sand until there was no sign of a hole.

Having tucked her bundle of eggs into the warm dune, the sea turtle dug her flippers into the sand and slowly wheeled around. She plodded straight for the water leaving a wide set of tracks. She reached the wet sand and tasted the sea. Waves broke over her crusty, old shell, and she kicked free of the land. The turtle dove into the face of the moon—a giant yellow moon sleeping on the sea. She didn't look back. She swam on and on.

Two raccoons prowling the dunes discovered the turtle nest. They dug through the sand and ate as many eggs as they could reach.

And what had been one hundred was now sixty-four.

Sixty-five days later, the baby turtles somehow knew it was time. Deep in the dark pit, the hatchlings ripped free of their eggshells and pushed and pulled in a wild scramble to the surface. The mass of baby turtles surged to the top, teeming over the rim of the nest like froth spilling from a boiling pot.

The hatchlings wasted no time. Without seeing the water, they saw that the light above the ocean was brighter, and they moved toward it. They streamed in small groups toward the sea, climbing up the hills and tumbling down the valleys of sand.

They scuttled across the face of the flat beach, marking the sand with hundreds of tiny tracks. The open beach was a dangerous place for small, soft turtles.

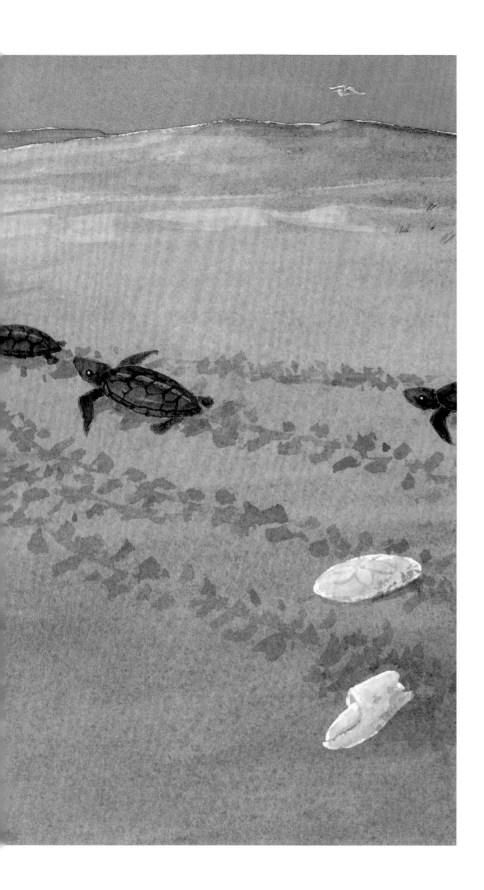

Ghost crabs with oversized pincers seized those hatchlings that came close to their underground burrows, and hauled them below.

And what had been one hundred was now twenty-two.

The sea turtle hatchlings reached the edge of the wet sand. Faster and faster the turtles crawled. A wave dashed onto the beach and scooped up the first batch of hatchlings. They tossed and spun in the wash and then rushed headlong into the surf.

A great blue heron flying over the breaking surf spotted the rush of hatchlings. The bird came to rest by the edge of the sea and plucked helpless turtles from the sand and water.

And what had been one hundred was now only ten.

The ten young turtles swam through the foam and froth of the sea, lighter than air. They popped to the surface to breathe, and down again they swam.

A sand shark cruised the shallow water and ripped through the band of little turtles, eating as many as it could see.

And what had been one hundred was now only two.

A pair of laughing gulls flew out to sea to bring fish back to their nesting young. They spied the thrashing water made by the fin of the feeding shark. One gull swooped low, snatched a hatchling in its beak, and swung back toward its nest.

And what had been one hundred was now only one.

The second gull spotted the last turtle and plucked it from the water. The bird turned to shore. A larger herring gull dove in to steal the prize and jammed its beak into the outstretched neck of the laughing gull. The small gull reeled and screamed, and the hatchling fell free. The big herring gull rolled to retrieve its prey, but the hatchling disappeared in the wash of breaking waves.

The sky turned red and gold as the sun rose over the edge of the earth. The lone sea turtle hatchling beat the waves with flying swim strokes. With its sea compass already fixed, the little turtle made straight for the open sea, pulled by a longing to be someplace far, far away.

And what had been one hundred was now one, following the ancient path to home.

About Sea Turtles

When the dinosaurs still roamed the land, over 100 million years ago, sea turtles swam through the earth's oceans, ancient reptiles in ancient seas. Though the dinosaurs have disappeared, sea turtles are still here — if just barely. There are five main kinds of sea turtle found in the oceans of the world. They are the leatherback, green, ridley, hawksbill and loggerhead. All are endangered.

There are many threats to sea turtles today. Nesting habitat is disappearing throughout the world as more and more beaches are developed. Thousands of turtles are drowned and killed when they get entangled in fishing gear. Trash such as plastic bags or balloons in the ocean is sometimes mistaken for food, such as jellyfish. Sea turtles eat this garbage, and it kills them by blocking their intestines. Artificial lights from houses and other buildings along the beach can confuse adult females and turtle hatchlings. The lights may attract baby turtles away from the ocean rather than toward it. In some countries,

Leatherback

Green

Ridley

Hawksbill

sea turtles are still hunted for their meat, shells, and eggs. And scientists are concerned about the alarming number of turtles affected by a disease that causes tumors. Scientists are searching for clues to what causes and spreads this disease.

The sea turtle in the story is a loggerhead, found in the warm waters of the Atlantic Ocean. Most species of sea turtles swim in the tropical seas of the Atlantic and Pacific Oceans. The leatherback, however, lives in cool temperate seas, as far north as Labrador and British Columbia. All sea turtles lay their eggs in a hole on the beach.

In many ways, sea turtles are mysteries. They are not easy to study. Most of the time the turtles are out of sight, under the sea, far from any human eye. Sometimes the only place to see them is on the beach.

The survival of the sea turtle is based on the number one hundred. The magic is in the math. Sea turtles produce on average one hundred eggs per nest. And a female may lay eggs in three or four nests, or sometimes more, in a season. It's an old formula that keeps the wild sea turtle populations alive.

One hundred eggs is enough to feed the ghost crabs, the wild hogs, and the hungry island raccoons. And when they've hatched, one hundred is enough to feed the gulls, the sharks, and the fish. Out of one hundred, maybe one turtle or two reach maturity. This is the story of one who did.

Loggerhead

Suggested Reading

There are two classic sea turtle books for older readers that tell a great story and are full of interesting sea turtle lore: *So Excellent a Fish – A Natural History of Sea Turtles* by Archie Carr (University of Texas Press, 1986) and *Time of the Turtle* by Jack Rudloe (Alfred A. Knopf, New York, 1979). Two books about sea turtles with color photos are *Sea Turtles* by Jeff Ripple (Voyageur Press, Worldlife Library, 2002) and *Sea Turtles of the World* by Doug Perrine (Voyageur Press, World Discovery Guides, 2003). Younger readers in grades 1 through 3 might want to read the following titles: *Sea Turtles* by Gail Gibbons (Holiday House, 1998) and *Into The Sea* by Brenda Guiberson (Henry Holt and Company, 2000).

Many thanks to Molly Lutcavage, Ph.D., New England Aquarium; Karen Bjorndal, Ph.D., Director of the Archie Carr Center for Sea Turtle Research, University of Florida; and Jerris Foote, Ph.D., Mote Marine Lab, for reviewing the manuscript and sharing their knowledge of sea turtles.

To Karen Hesse, thank you for the title, and thank you for believing in my writing so many years ago. And to every scientist, researcher, and naturalist helping to save sea turtles, a world of gratitude. Future generations will be happy you did.
—S.R.S.

To my Uncle Fred, a great man of letters, both kinds.
—B.H.

Boyds Mills Press, Inc.
815 Church Street
Honesdale, Pennsylvania 18431
Printed in the United States of America

Library of Congress Cataloging-in-Publication Data

Swinburne, Stephen R.
Turtle tide : the ways of sea turtles / by Stephen R. Swinburne ; illustrated by Bruce Hiscock.— 1st ed.
p. cm.
ISBN 978-1-59078-081-7 (hc) • ISBN 978-1-59078-827-1 (pb)
1. Sea turtles—Juvenile literature. I. Hiscock, Bruce, ill. II. Title.

QL666.C536S95 2005   597.92'8—dc22
2004016856

First edition
First Boyds Mills Press paperback edition, 2010
The text of this book is set in 14-point Minion.
The illustrations are done in watercolor.

10 9 8 7 6 5 (hc)
10 9 8 7 6 5 4 3 2 1 (pb)